Author Biographies

A. A. Milne

Charlotte Guillain

www.raintreepublishers.co.uk
Visit our website to find out more information about Raintree books.

To order:
☎ Phone 0845 6044371
📄 Fax +44 (0) 1865 312263
💻 Email myorders@raintreepublishers.co.uk

Customers from outside the UK please telephone +44 1865 312262

Raintree is an imprint of Capstone Global Library Limited, a company incorporated in England and Wales having its registered office at 7 Pilgrim Street, London, EC4V 6LB – Registered company number: 6695582

Edited by Rebecca Rissman, Daniel Nunn, and Sian Smith
Designed by Joanna Hinton-Malivoire
Picture research by Tracy Cummins
Production by Victoria Fitzgerald
Originated by Capstone Global Library Ltd
Printed and bound in China by South China Printing Company Ltd

ISBN 978 1 406 23449 7
15 14 13 12 11
10 9 8 7 6 5 4 3 2 1

British Library Cataloguing in Publication Data
Guillain, Charlotte.
A.A. Milne. – (Author biographies)
1. Milne, A. A. (Alan Alexander), 1882-1956–Pictorial works–Juvenile literature. 2. Authors, English-20th century–Biography–Pictorial works–Juvenile literature.
I. Title II. Series
823.9'12-dc22

Acknowledgements
Alamy pp.7 (© Stunning images), 18 (© david We would like to thank the following for permission to reproduce photographs: Alamy Images pp. 7 (© Stunning images), 18, 23d (© david hancock), 20 (© Moviestore Collection Ltd), 21 (© Richard Sheppard); Corbis pp. 6 (© The Francis Frith Collections), 8 (© E.O. Hoppé), 14 (© Bettmann); Getty Images pp. 4, 12 (Hulton Archive), 11 (Apic), 15, 23a (Mike Coppola), 16 (David Montgomery), 17 (Evening Standard); NARA p. 23g (War & Conflict CD); Penguin Group (USA) Inc. pp. 5, 10, 13, 23f; Photographers Direct p. 9 (Lebrecht Music & Arts Photo Library); Shutterstock pp. 23b (© Tatiana Popova), 23c (© Iuchunyu), 23e (© Graeme Dawes); The Royal Borough of Kensington and Chelsea p. 19 (Virtual Museum).

Cover photograph of Alan Alexander Milne with his son Christopher Robin Milne reproduced with permission of Getty Images (Apic). Back cover photograph of the toys that inspired the writing of Winnie-the-Pooh reproduced with permission of Getty Images (Mike Coppola).

Every effort has been made to contact copyright holders of material reproduced in this book. Any omissions will be rectified in subsequent printings if notice is given to the publisher.

Contents

Some words are shown in bold, **like this**. You can find them in the glossary on page 23.

Who was A. A. Milne?

A. A. Milne was a writer.

He wrote stories and **poems** for children.

His full name was Alan Alexander Milne.

His most famous book is called
Winnie-the-Pooh.

Where did he grow up?

A. A. Milne was born in 1882.

He lived in London, England.

Westminster School

A. A. Milne grew up in the school where his father was a teacher.

Then he went to a famous school in London.

What did he do before he was a writer?

World War 1 started in 1914.

A. A. Milne joined the army and went to fight in France.

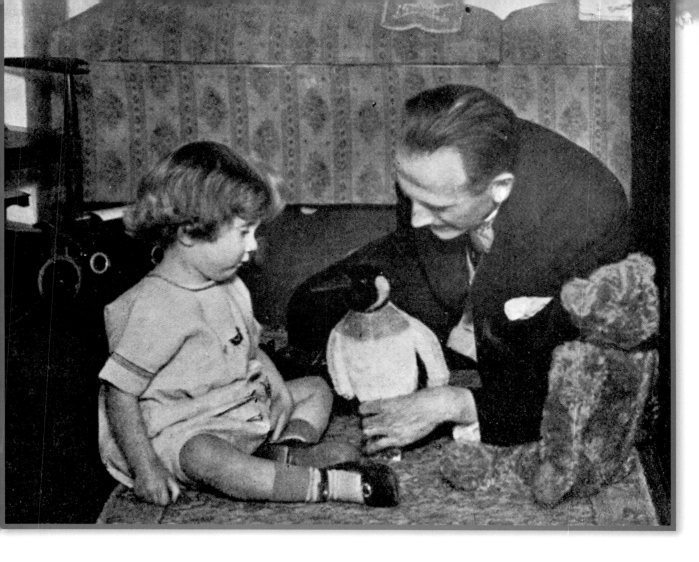

After the war, A. A. Milne returned home to write **plays**.

Then he had a son called Christopher Robin.

How did he start writing books?

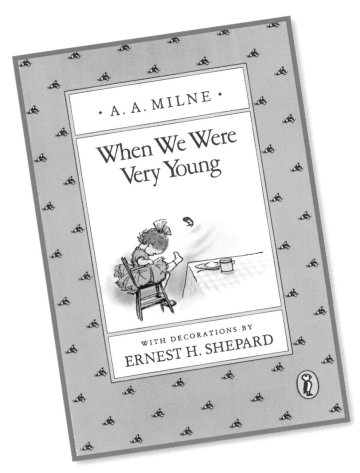

A. A. Milne wrote poetry for children that was **published** in magazines.

His **poems** were put together in a book called *When We Were Very Young*.

Then he wrote a book of stories called *Winnie-the-Pooh*.

Winnie-the-Pooh was Christopher Robin's toy bear.

What books did he write?

A. A. Milne wrote two other books for children.

The House at Pooh Corner was also about Winnie-the-Pooh and his friends.

Now We Are Six was another **collection** of **poems**.

A. A. Milne also wrote some **plays** for adults.

What did he write about?

A. A. Milne's poetry was usually funny.

His **poems** were often about young children exploring the world.

A. A. Milne's stories were about his son Christopher Robin.

Christopher Robin's toy animals were also in these funny stories.

Who drew the pictures in A. A. Milne's books?

A. A. Milne did not draw the pictures in his books.

Ernest H. Shepard was an artist who drew the pictures.

Some of Ernest's pictures are black and white **line drawings**.

Other pictures are painted in colour.

What else did A. A. Milne do?

A. A. Milne also wrote films and **plays**.

He used the book *The Wind in the Willows* to write a play called *Toad of Toad Hall*.

A. A. Milne was not well when he got older.

He liked living in the country and reading books.

Why is he famous today?

People still buy A. A. Milne's books today.

Many children see his characters in cartoon films and on television.

You can see toys of these characters in the shops.

People still write books and magazines about them, too.

Timeline of A. A. Milne's life and work

1882   A. A. Milne was born in London.

1916   A. A. Milne went to France to fight in **World War 1**.

1920   Christopher Robin was born.

1924   *When We Were Very Young* was **published**.

1926   *Winnie-the-Pooh* was published.

1927   *Now We Are Six* was published.

1928   *The House at Pooh Corner* was published.

1956   A. A. Milne died.

Glossary

collection group of things put together

line drawing picture made of dark lines, done with a pen or pencil

play story that is acted out

poem piece of writing that puts ideas or feelings into words. Some poems rhyme.

published made into a book or put in a magazine and printed

World War 1 a big war that lasted for more than four years

Find out more

Books

Books by A. A. Milne and E.H. Shepard: *When We Were Very Young, Winnie-the-Pooh, Now We Are Six,* and *The House at Pooh Corner.*

Websites

www.poohcorner.com
Visit this website to find out more about A. A. Milne and Christopher Robin.

Index